Forex Trading;

The Beginners Guide To Smashing Pips Trading, Tips to Successful Trading, Trading Mindset, Trading Psychology, Forex Mastery,

By

Charles T Mercer

Contents

Foreword

The aim of this book is to give readers a brief overview on Forex markets, the smart methods to use and the ideas to scrap.

I've been Forex Trading for 20 years, firstly in New York and now in central London. Trading Forex has never been easier with apps and trading platforms readily available for every phone, mac and PC. However this doesn't mean trading is easy. There are two vital facets to trading. The first is the skills to trade. This is actually something which like any other trade or skill should be honed and worked on to continually improve. Your trade training and knowledge should never end. The saying, knowledge is power certainly applies here.

The second element would be developing the mindset of a trader. The means through which traders can develop the proper mentality when trading, why emotional management is critical to successfully trading on the Forex market.

These aspects of Forex trading will be discussed in depth in the other chapters that follow but for now, we tackle the basics pertaining to Forex trading as a money making entity.

Let's begin our Forex Trading journey.

What Is Forex?

Forex is short for foreign exchange, and is a $4 trillion a day world-wide business where can make huge profit...and huge loss. People's lives can change for the better or worse in a big way. Foreign exchange is the act of changing one country's currency into another country's currency for a variety of reasons, usually for tourism or commerce.

Currency trading was really limited to interbank activity on behalf of their clients. Gradually, the banks themselves set up proprietary desks to trade for their own accounts, and this was followed by large multi-national corporations, hedge funds and high net worth individuals.

With the explosion of the internet, a retail market aimed at individual traders has sprung up that provides easy access to the foreign exchange markets.

Now we can trade on our home computer and mobile phone anywhere in the world.

Forex trading can be particularly unstable to the untrained eye. It is dictated by many connective elements around the world. Things like war, oil prices, and global shifts in power are just a few of the elements that effect the forex movements. For example look at 'Brexit' which was a vote to for Britain to leave the European market. This had a direct effect on the GB currency. Smart traders took advantage of this. However most times these changes are not immediate but gradual over time.

The Basics

There are many companies that are successfully trading in the forex. For them, forex trading has no off days, holidays or time offs. These companies run on 24 hour cycles no matter which part of the world they may be located in.

Forex trading also has its fair share of scams and to avoid this it would be prudent to do some research on which broker to use, and especially before taking the word of the forex traders and investing a lot of money on the here say or speculation of a few people. There are no magic formulas and every trade has the accompanying risks.

There are also many career opportunities in the forex trading line. Most large forex trading companies hire a varied amount of people to trade. Individual traders, brokers and bank to bank transactions are the most common and accepted ways of trading. The statistic taken last year showed the trading volume reached about 4 trillion USD per day.

Besides the daily transactions for profits, there are also other uses that require some lever of forex movements. These other users may include wages paid to foreign banks for multinational personnel.

However a large percentage of trading is more for profits which can be rather considerable.

Where Forex Trading Takes Place

In the past, Forex trading was exclusively conducted by hedge funds, central banks, multinational currency companies, and major banks however; this has changed in recent times due the latest surge in internet development and market innovations allowing even the small time trader the opportunity to participate in the Forex market.

Some Forex broker companies offer a variety of accounts to their clients enabling retail traders the chance to trade in relatively smaller lots.

Even though Forex markets have undergone some remarkable improvement, it still remains largely unregulated; and Forex trading rules have not yet been clearly defined especially when trades go beyond international borders.

Furthermore, traders with a sizeable amount of risk capital as is the case with hedge funds and banks which have the ability to influence the Forex market due to their huge financial leverage; therefore, those with little or no experience in Forex trade will be venturing into risky unchartered territories.

In as much as Forex trading carries very high risks, traders who go through the trouble of educating themselves on the whole process could quite easily make a huge fortune in just a few weeks, with those doing the contrary getting disastrous results amounting to huge losses.

What is The New York Stock Exchange

Some documentations list the beginnings of the NYSE or the New York Stock Exchange to begin in May 17th 1792. At the time of its humble beginnings it only had about 24 stock brokers working together to form the stock brokerage. All this was and still is, on the street called Wall Street.

As it expanded over the years it has changed locations but has retained the "wall street" tag. It is known to be the largest stock trading house in the world and at last statistical count it was listed to be trading daily at about $153 billion. The statistics also showed that at one time it had a market capitalization of its listed companies at the huge figure of $13.39 trillion. These are all mind boggling figures and it is rather amazing to note the shear amount of paper transactions that are done on a minute to minute basis.

Platform

This powerful form of trading which is facilitated by the NYSE provides the platform for buyers and sellers to trade shares of stock in companies registered with the board for public trading. Keeping to the age old working time frame of a five day working week of Monday to Friday, its runs from 9.30am – 4.00pm, closing only for holidays previously set and declared by the Exchange in advance.

Though when first observed it can seem quite chaotic and loud, there is an underlying system in place which is very familiar to all on the trading floor. The "buying and selling" is done at a very fast and energetic pace and the alertness of an individual plays an extremely big role in getting the transactions done according to requirements of clients or customers. These "customers" or clients usually appoint brokers to do the trading on their behalf sometimes with specific guidelines and some leaving the decisions to the discretion of the brokers hired.

What Is Traded?

In very basic terms the stock market is where buyers and sellers meet and decide on a price for a particular commodity. There has to be a willing seller and a willing buyer for the transaction to be successfully completed. Previously these transactions were done at physical locations but now with the advancement of technology, now these transactions can be done virtually.

What Changes Hands

Typically the trading floor tends to consists of traders seemingly chaotically waving their hand around wildly while shouting out various instructions and messages. Then there is the more sedate style of trading where everything is done electronically with a network of computers. And further down there is a person at home or even on the bus setting up a trade on their phone.

Also simply described as the facilitating of exchange of securities between buyers and sellers it plays a certain role in reducing the risks of investing. It also provides for the arena for all interested parties to be able to conduct the relevant transactions of buying and selling.

The instructions to buy and sell stocks in a particular company will be given through a brokerage firm. This information will be passed on to those on the trading floor with the intention of linking the agreed price and commodity to the buyer and seller.

When this partnership is identified and the transaction exercise beings the virtual trading begins. Sometimes this is all done within a matter of seconds and can involve a huge amount of money.

There are several different categories of stocks traded at any given time frame. These may include common stock and preferred stock. As it denotes the common stock is an individual's representation of a company and a claim to its profits made. The ownership of the stock allows the individual to vote on a per share basis to elect the board members but have no direct "say" over the decisions made within the company. As for preferred stock holders, this group does represent some degree of ownership but without the same voting rights and in the event of liquidation this group is paid off first, next only to the debtors.

What Are Forex Pairs?

Though most transactions are done virtually the money involved is very real indeed, because a lot of these transactions involve buyers and sellers of different nations. Thus, the need to transact using duel currency or otherwise known as forex currency pairs.

The Pairs

Basically it means buying stocks in one currency and then simultaneously selling the same already purchased stock in another currency. Both these currencies will be clearly stipulated alongside each transaction for the perusal and knowledge of both buyer and seller.

Some of the more commonly used pairs are often divided into two categories of major and minor currencies. Major currencies are the most popularity used traded currencies which are USD, EUR, JPY, GBP, CHF, CAD and AUD, while NZD and ZAR are considered the minor currencies.

There are also circumstances that don't require the common forex pairs to be used and instead other parings are allowed such as the replacement of USD with EUR, GBP, or AUD against other currencies. These types of transactions are commonly known as quote currency exchange.

Among the more popular pairings are:

- EUR – USD
- USD – JPY
- GBP – USD
- USD – CHF
- EUR – CHF
- AUD – USD
- NZD – GBP

These forex trading pairs are a general trading tool for the many currencies of the world and are currently rising as the largest and least regulated market providing the greatest liquidity to investers globally.

Simply put, it is buying a certain currency or commodity at a lower rate and then when there is a currency fluctuation that is advantageous to the seller then said purchase is sold for a profit. Some consider this type of trading to be very volatile and risky but if done well the profits can be rather significant.

Inversely you can sell a currency if you have worked out it will drop and make a similar profit.

Market Size And Liquidity

There are several features that make the foreign exchange market rather unique and a little complicated. Thus it is not really a suitable endeavor for the faint hearted.

Among the elements it involves are the actual trading which is done in large volumes, the extreme liquidity conditions of the market, the large number and variety of traders and commodities available at any given time, the geographical dispersion of its participants, the long trading hours.

The aspect that makes all these so volatile is the variety of possible effects the exchange rates can have on the actual trading or transactions.

Inside Info

The various markets size trading could run in the billion to the trillions and the liquidity factor are also high in terms of percentages.

These market size participations run on a daily average turn over which is always significantly high even if it does not include global trading exercises.

Being the most liquid financial market in the world its traders include major banking houses, central banks, institutional investors, currency speculators, corporations, governments and retail investors.

As stated before this style of trading is very volatile indeed. In being so the profound effects of the currency market is almost always unpredictable. Political climates, international trading relationships, events and other underlying factor may contribute to the volatility and the possible liquidity rations involved.

All these various aspects contribute to the uniqueness of the market and its liquidity. An unfathomable number of traders and transactions are possible within a 24 hour time window.

In comparison with other markets, trading the exchange rate settings are with fairly low net margins. Some may even consider it the real market for perfect competition even with all the possible risks.

All these factor into the liquidity of the trading environment. Liquidity is a very important element because it determines how easily the price can change. This liquidity element of the forex trading enables huge trading volumes to occur with little effort but a lot of skill.

What Is A Spot Market?

There are many terms that are linked to the forex trading environment. One of which is the term spot market. This term refers to the commodities or securities market where items or goods are sold for cash and then immediately delivered.

All of this is done with a deliberate intention of getting the best transactions done. The contracts are bought and sold during the trading on the markets and are usually deemed immediately effective.

Spot

Then there is the futures transaction which is where the commodities can be purchased and expected to be delivered in a short and specific time frame. Being a forward moving physical market this form of transaction are bought and sold at spot prices.

The spot market is also sometimes referred to as a cash market or physical market because the prices are settled in cast at the time the transaction is agreed upon. This immediate form of buying and selling is sometimes considered more effective as opposed to forward pricing conditions.

A good example to use to portray this spot market transaction is the crude oil trading. The crude oil transaction is done on a future's statistics but is sold on spot prices and its physical delivery is done within a short time frame previously stipulated and agreed upon. Also to be noted is that these spot trading style transactions are done immediately as opposed to having the convenience of a longer time frame for settling the "account".

Because of the time frame element involved, spot trading is almost opposite to futures contracts in quite a few significant ways. The spot trading style usually expires well before any physical delivery of goods.

The most common kind of spot trading is the foreign exchange. There are normally compensations expected if the time frame given for settling the value of the transaction immediately is not met. The transaction compensation is for the time value and duration delay for delivery. Since these transactions are settled electronically, the forex market is essentially instantaneous.

What Is Futures Trading?

When it comes to finance, the standardized contract between two consenting parties is part of the exchange of a specific asset which has been certified for its quantity and quality for a price agreed. Both the price and the delivery are specified and the future delivery date is noted, thus the contracts are considered future exchanges.

Futures

In the futures trading both the buyer and the seller have opposing intentions in the idea behind the transactions. The seller hopes the price will drop after the transaction has been concluded whereas the buyer hopes for the rise in the price to ensure a profit from the transaction.

It should be noted that all the transactions need not always be about commodities. There are also underlying assets to a futures contract which may include financial futures, securities or financial instruments and intangible assets or referenced items such as stock indexes and interest rates.

Futures trading help to facilitate the transactions of the exchange institution as intermediary while minimizing the risks of default by either party within the transaction frame.

Margin

The term margin refers to the initial amount of cash required by both parties to be deposited and settled on a daily basis as dictated by the fluctuations of the market sentiments.

This process is done on an automatic basis where the changes in pricing is taken form one account and deposited into the other account between buyer and seller. When the said margin goes below a certain stipulated amount then there is a call to top up the deleted amount in order to keep the transaction account running.

In the futures trading there is also another term popularly used which signifies another type of transaction. This is called the forward contract. This forward contract is like a futures one but has very specific definitions in each category. All prices and commodities and time frames are locked and thus there is no need for the margin style settlement practice.

What Are Options Trading?

In understanding options trading one will realize the many advantages to this type of trading investment. This type of trading known as options trading gives the individual the flexibility to speculate and place what is perceived to be informed bets to garner very specific outcomes in terms of profits.

Options

This will allow the investor to purchase commodities in various forms and hold them for a set period of time then when deemed fit the trading either above or below a certain price will commence, depending which way the bet or speculation favors.

These option trading styles also provide enormous amounts of leverage for the participating traders. Thus with only a relatively small investment an options trader can control a very significant underlying stock position.

The risks involved are very high indeed as are the profits. Before an individual decides to dabble in this style of profiting, serious consideration should be given to the possible consequences of an unwise investment choice.

Understanding the fundaments involved in the options trading foray will help to ensure minimalistic loses. There are times when certain stocks are over inflated, thus by having some level of in depth knowledge on how the options trading is run the individual is less likely to be caught in such a scenario.

The versatility offered by the options trading style can be quite attractive then thus be a great pulling factor to potential investors.

However because of the complexities involved in the securities and also the extreme risk factors caution is always advised.

Some people may decide the options trading is not for them and thus avoid it altogether, however in doing so, one may be depriving one's self of a possible beneficial windfall. Having a little knowledge in this area, can also be beneficial in helping the individual with other forms of investments, as these investments may have some connections to options trading.

What Are Exchange-traded Funds?

Quite a few exchange traded funds have started in the trading scene. In some parts of the world it has managed to gain a fairly healthy foot hold while in other parts of the world it is still looked at with a little trepidation.

Exchange Trade

Understanding what exchange traded funds are and its basic fundamental workings is instrumental in being able to successfully invest in it. One should be well aware of the workings, risks, and benefits this type of investment can provide.

When compared to traditional unit trust funds where the sell order is transacted at the fund's net asset value, the exchange trade funds are traded with the similar style but with the advantage of incurring lower costs.

Also another advantage is that the exchange traded funds conditions provide for the non-requirement of having to pay an entry fee. Thus another benefit in terms of cost, in the option to investing in exchange trade funds.

Some may view the risks factor are much lower as compared to going into the investment foray on an individual basis. The exchange trade funds are more cost effective as the means of acquiring the proposed investments are done not only by trained professional with a considerable amount of knowledge in the field of investing, but also done as a "basket of stocks" – meaning a wide variety of stocks, rather than going with one particular option only.

The wise use of the exchange trade funds allows for the decreased but still ever present risks factors.

The exchange traded funds are also more cost effective as the intentions encouraged would be to "hold" the acquired portfolio for a long period of time. Thus the need to be constantly in touch with the very volatile market movements is effectively eliminated, and some level of peace of mind is touted.

The Dangers Of Trading?

The end goal of forex trading is to yield a net profit by buying low and selling high. Forex traders have the advantage of choosing a handful of currencies over stock traders who must parse thousands of companies and sectors

Leverage Risks

In forex trading, leverage requires a small initial investment, called a margin, to gain access to substantial trades in foreign currencies. Small price fluctuations can result in margin calls, where the investor is required to pay an additional margin. Volatile market conditions will result in substantial losses in excess of initial investments.

Interest Rate Risks

In basic macroeconomics courses you learn that interest rates have an effect on countries' exchange rates. If a country's interest rates rise, its currency will strengthen due to an influx of investments in that country's assets putatively because a stronger currency provides higher returns. Conversely, if interest rates fall, its currency will weaken as investors begin to withdraw their investments

Transaction Risks

Transaction risks are an exchange rate risk associated with time differences between the beginning of a contract and when it settles. Forex trading occurs on a 24 hour basis which can result in exchange rates changing before trades have settled. Consequently, currencies may be traded at different prices at different times during trading hours.

While forex assets have the highest trading volume, the risks are apparent and can lead to severe losses.

Forex trading must be acknowledged and properly understood. Thousands of people have become rich and even more have lost everything to this volatile and unforgiving way of investing.

Caution First

Sometimes the investor himself or herself can be their own worst enemy. There are innumerable inexperienced traders who have put on a trade, seen it go the wrong way, and when the pain is too much they close the trade at a loss.

Then the trade will actually play out the way it should of and you would've actually made money on it. Even traders with a strategy will make this mistake.
On top of that you could be affected by tiredness, boredom, taking it too easy, not focused on the market movement and many more. All of these various distractions can cause detrimental and irreversible damage. Being too adventurous can also bite you hard.

Then there are also the outside forces of the market itself, which may cause the unforeseen problems that cause the investments to decrease in value. One may have applied all the right methods and formulas but if the markets takes a turn for the worst then most investments are like to suffer too. Many factors like unseen or unexpected political problems, the shifts in power within companies, secret mergers, and alliances are some of the elements that may not be privy or common knowledge to the ordinary person.

The Mindset and Trading

Forex trading can be highly lucrative especially if you are equipped with the necessary trading knowledge and skills. Apart from possessing trading skills, it is essential to have the right mindset for you to be successful in Forex trading.

This is the crucial aspect where most traders fail. No matter how good you are in utilizing various trading strategies without the right mindset, you might not be able to achieve the desired results.

Some would think that trading success happens in an instant and that they can easily make money out of it overnight. Although there is some truth in this belief and it is not next to impossible, only those who continuously develop effective trading habits coupled with the right trading mindset can actually prosper. Here are the best tips that you can use to ensure success in Forex trading.

Step 1: Set Realistic Expectations

The initial step is to set realistic expectations. Of course, all people would want to earn profit. In this kind of business where currency trading is highly volatile, you win some and you lose some. Chances are, if you use the right strategies and forecast, you can definitely earn a huge sum. But on the other hand, you can also lose your money.

Basically the point here is to hope for the best outcome and anticipate the worst case scenario. There are still many factors and other market forces that can directly and indirectly affect currency trading. Make sure that you do not stake your whole life on the line just to be in the Forex trading business. It is strongly suggested that you trade using disposable risk capital, spare money that you can use for any trading ventures.

Step 2: Trade Wisely- Quality over Quantity

It is a common misconception of some traders that they have to trade everyday just to optimize their earnings. The truth of the matter is that, you can further elevate your earnings if you learn how to be patient in trading. Patience is a key skill to success. If you really want to achieve long term success and get to explore the markets, you need to learn how to trade using daily charts.

Along with learning how to properly use these daily charts to your advantage, you start to develop your trading mindset where you have to patiently wait for the right timing. Once you have calculated the risks, worked out why you are entering, then that is the perfect time to make the decision.

Step 3: Be Organized in Your Approach

Learning the market forces that affect the movements in any trading system takes a while. Without any organized approach, you might end up losing your money. Before anything else, you need to come up with your own trading plan and trading journal.

This allows you to trade with discipline and to be more organized when it comes to your trading activities and trading options. Monitoring your daily trading journal enables you to assess your performance and monitor your earnings as well.

Last but not the least, use the price data and other relevant information before you trade. Be decisive in your trading decisions and always go for calculated risks.

How To Trade On The Forex

Since Forex is by far the most popular trading world of currency, it also connotes that one should be able to understand the factors involved in the trading process to truly garner profit from it. If you were one of the people who want to fit in and moreover, standout in this market, then some of the tips below would help you get a head start.

Understanding the Jargons of the Market

Jargons are basically the terms used in a certain company. To be able to understand the whole process, then one should take the time to integrate what the terms mean.

The basic of these are:

'Base currency' - the term for the currency one is spending or is trying to get rid of. This works primarily by selling one currency so you can actually buy another type of it.

'Exchange rate' - is the term you look at when you want to know how much you would spend to buy base currency from your quote currency.

These are just some of the terms found in Forex trading.

It is also important for you to decide on the two primary currencies that you want to buy and sell. Thus, just like any other businesses, you should be consistent in the quality of your task. Therefore, staying at one exchange rate would possibly entail bigger profits.

Opening an Account

A brokerage account is an important part of the exchanging currency business. You firstly have to consider the reliability of the broker you choose to open an account to. It is advisable to research about the broker's background and how many years they been in the industry. In addition to this, you should also be able to identify the broker's transparency through asking some of the people that also has an account. Also look at reviews on the net and ask other traders who they use. This is very easy on social media.

Start your Trade!

This step is the most important part of this business. Once you started your venture and has done steps 1 and 2 for preparatory, be not complacent and still take time to analyze the market before you proceed to the trade itself. Preparation as for anything important in life, is again the key to success. Like a sniper preparing to take a shot, getting in the right position, waiting, using the surroundings to his advantage and readying himself. Entering the trade is like pulling the trigger. It is the final part of the trade.

The technical, fundamental and sentiment analyses should be considered.

- Technical means reviewing and researching on charts regarding the previous action of the currency.
- Fundamental is taking a bird's eye view of the economic fundamentals of different countries, and thus using this to your advantage in choosing the right currencies.
- Sentiment analysis entails the mood of the market.

Never forget that every step you take can lead to the destruction or the progress of your trading. It is good to take risks but it is better to always be cautious about it. Move slowly. Do not just engage in this trading venture because you thought it will be easy and would be a get rich quick idea. Every step must be counted and therefore must be taken into full consideration.

If you take the risks with the proper weapons of knowledge, you can take the right shot and hit the mark.

Have Realistic Expectations

Starting out in Forex trade is never an easy thing. With the promise of high investment returns, a lot of people are easily enticed to venture in currency trade without having second thoughts. After all, who would not want to double or to triple their money? For some, this might appear as the easiest way for financial liberation. Forex trading can definitely make it possible for you to earn more.

When you come across Forex trading websites, almost all would promise you converting your money into millions in just a short span of time. Some online advertisements would even beguile you to finally quit your job and to just focus on Forex trading.

But is it really worth it?

Why Set Realistic Expectations

The answer is both a yes and a no. Forex trading is definitely worth your effort especially when you already possess the right mindset and you use effective trading strategies. But the promise of earning thousands or even millions overnight is just impossible and even dangerous.

When you finally set to venture in currency trade, setting realistic expectations is the initial step. Success in this kind of business all starts with knowing what to actually expect. Since there are different market forces that can directly and indirectly impact currency trade, you can never be 100% sure.

Always keep in mind that any investment involves certain risks. It is basically the same thing when it comes to Forex trading. Without a doubt, you can earn a huge sum. But on the other side, you can also incur losses. Once you come out thinking that you can have all the economic gains by just buying and selling currencies, you are doomed to fail. Remember that just like in kind of investment venture, you need to be realistic to make your goals achievable and feasible. Your attitude and mindset towards Forex trading certainly affect your trading decisions.

Calculating Risks in Forex

Instilling impossible expectations towards Forex profitability can negatively affect your trading choices. For one, traders who have high and impractical expectations might end up gambling their money without even thinking of the risks.

The tendency is that some would easily want to get high profits in an instant. There are even traders who would trade currencies everyday thinking that by doing so, they can earn more. With Forex trading being a highly volatile business venture, you can never afford to trade without even calculating the risks and without any Forex knowledge. Doing so will not only lead to disappointment but to high losses as well.

If you really want to make it in this kind of business, you need to have patience. You have to set realistic expectations so that you can carefully plan your trading strategies. Study the currency market, gather the price data along with the significant indicators and create your trading plan. These are the things that you should keep in mind if you really want to be successful in Forex.

With Forex trading, patience is definitely a virtue. You need to know when to use your bullets to your advantage. In that way, you can avoid incurring losses and you begin on your journey to earn high profits.

Understand The Power Of Patience

A lot of people make huge losses in Forex markets just because they make simple mistakes like overtrading or not being patient enough to allow their trade setups to play out and instead they enter and exit the Forex market compulsively. The problem may lie not so much with your trading strategy but with your inability to exercise patience by waiting for the best low risk opportunity with the highest probability of success. The tips discussed below will help any trader step up their trades from mediocre trading to consistent and profitable trades.

Educate Yourself on the Forex Market

It is important that new traders educate themselves on all matters concerning the Forex Market resisting the impulse to rush into trades before understanding the ins and outs of the trade. The why you entered trade is more important than anything. Always enter a trade and be ready to answer a question from someone who says why did you do that? What was the reason for entering that trade? When I first started I couldn't give a technical answer. It's not enough to say I thought the price would go up. Why did you think that? The more reasons you have, the less risk you have.

Learning through mistakes on the Forex market could leave you counting your losses, but lucky for you this can be avoided by taking the time to study the market. Create a demo account and practice. After clearly establishing your trading knowledge, you can now exercise patience by waiting for the right moment to execute your trade; patience is worthless unless the trader knows what they are waiting for.

Create a Trading Plan and Stick to It

The best traders in the market always plan ahead and are prepared at all times having compiled an elaborate trading plan after which they always act according to their plans. They look at the market the night before and look at upcoming news events.

Creating a plan does not necessarily mean that they trade all the time; novice traders usually accumulate losses because they think that they should be on the market trading all the time. Preparation is an important aspect to any successful trade but at times it's better to sit tight and wait for the trade to play out; just because the Forex market is open 24/7 does not mean that you should be trading all the time.

Wait for Your Trade Setup to Play Out

Good traders never anticipate how their trades will play out, those who do lose a lot of money in this manner. Exercise patience when your trade plays out and bear in mind that a good trader can be compared to a lion, an amazing predator due to his great stalking skills, and a patient one at that, always waiting for the perfect opportunity to go for the kill and what's more when he goes for it he rarely misses.

A great trader once said that big money is made by sitting and waiting, and never by thinking, he adds that it's important to wait for all the factors to tilt in your favor prior to making the trade.

Be Organized in Your Approach to the Markets

The phrase "playing the market" may make it seem like you would enjoy greater success by trusting your gut instincts, going with the flow, and being a slave to trends. However, the truth is actually the opposite. You have better chances of earning from Forex trading if you adapt a more disciplined and organized method when trading.

Avoid letting your emotions and all the hype get the better of you with the following tips.

Planning is still the key to success

If you remember your Management 101 lessons, then you should know that Planning is the first step to success. Forex trading is no exception. You need to come up with plans for your short-term and long-term goals. These plans also have to be detailed. If possible, include step-by-step guidelines for how you want your strategy to work out. Pin these strategies to the wall with your trading computer. You can then keep reminding yourself what your initial plans were.

Focus on a few high-potential currency pairs.

Don't spread your resources thin. It's hard to put your plan and strategies to good use when you have a lot on your plate. Rather, it's better to take your time choosing a small number of currency pairs that you can fully focus on and nurture until the very end.

The more time you spend studying how your pair works in the market, the more chances you have of predicting its future trends. So for example just look at US – JPN. You can learn what affects this currency, what day's news reports come up and affect this currency. Soon you'll know it back to front. Consequently, you'll have a lesser need to rely on instincts alone when making a decision. Instinct is not a bad thing at all, but instincts powered by knowledge are even more trustworthy.

Use a timetable

A timetable can be a more powerful tool than an ordinary calendar if you know how to make good use of it. To start with, take note of all the important events that are relevant to your trading plan and strategies. These include but are not limited to the following:

- Public holidays in both countries where your currency pairs originate
- Global and economic summits affecting your currency pairs
- Economic releases

- Scheduled key announcements from major market players

All the events above are sure to affect your currency pair in terms of demand, supply, and liquidity – just to name a few. Every time you add an event to your timetable, remember to review your plan and strategies and adjust them accordingly if it proves necessary.

Expand your network.

When it comes to any kind of trading, it's who you know, what you know, and when you know that matter. Being able to predict market trends is a great skill, but it's not one you can always rely on. However, what you can be sure to depend on at all times is your network. It's fairly easy to determine which individuals will make good sources for insider's information. The challenges lie in making those individuals a willing part of your network. There are many people on Instagram and twitter you can follow. Also there are countless videos on youtube to watch that give you specific strategies.

Check technical analyses.

Technical opinions must always be taken into account even if you strongly feel the opposite of what these experts have to say. At the end of the day, you need to remind yourself that technical analyses are based on verifiable facts and figures.

Last but not the least, remember that your ultimate goal is to minimize your loss first and increase your profit next. Don't gamble.

Be man enough to admit when you're on the losing side and just start again. At least you still have something to start with unlike other traders, who have lost everything because of their inability to keep their emotions in check.

Why Emotional Management is Critical to Trading Success

Trading in the foreign exchange market is not all about strategies. Oftentimes, it can involve a lot of emotions especially when the experience is not at all pleasant. After all, even when the system of trading is reliable, human factor still remains as the major player. The trader can be very effective in maximizing the potentials of the trading system.

It is also possible that the trader might lack certain qualities that prevent him in making the right approaches. It becomes even more disadvantageous when the trader lacks patience in dealing with losing trades. Thus, it is essential to control strong emotional urges ensure that the process of trading is managed properly.

Proper Emotion Management can Lead to Better Calls

There are instances wherein a trader dismisses the signs that his ways are inefficient, thinking that it is the system that is at fault. When this happens, the trader will continue with the trade, hoping that the system will eventually turn out for the better. On the part of the trader, this kind of reaction can be translated to as being optimistic. However, unless the trader is already an expert in the Forex market and he has the right resources that will validate his moves, this reaction is actually an act of stubbornness more than anything else.

The trader is given two paths- to recognize what is happening or to maintain blind optimism. When the trader recognizes that the pattern is not going to favor his end anytime soon, the best decision would be to cut losses short. Acknowledging the technicalities of how the market works will prevent the trader from experiencing any more marginal losses.

It is quite observed from novice traders that they are too hopeful when they enter the Forex market. Although optimism can be a good thing, failure to identify negative signs while they are happening will undeniably slow down the trader's progress in this volatile industry.

Patience Yields Better Results

On the other side of the spectrum, it is also important to keep emotions in check when good things are happening during the trade. However, a normal reaction from a trader who is new to the system and has immediately acquired profit would be to withdraw them at the first sign. After all, liquidating the profits will translate to guaranteed earnings.

A good lesson that amateur traders can get from experts in the system would be to let their profits run. It is true that seeing the first sign of profits will make a novice trader excited to cash out on his earnings, but if he really wants to succeed in the system, he should learn how to play along with it.

With familiarity, guidance and patience, the trader can still expand his profits while letting it run its course. The trader can study past trends so it will be easier for him to recognize the signs that the market is about to reverse. Once this occurs, he can liquidate his profits which he allowed to mature to its best potential.

Taking The First Step

So we have reached the end of my trading book. To make trading work you should firstly be using a demo account. This is where you can learn your skills, learn about what makes a currency move the way it does. It is better to make your demo amount the same amount of money that you will eventually put in.

To do this you need to find a brokerage first. Research brokers online, read reviews, ideally a company in your country that abides by the trading laws.

You need to develop as a trader, to know the business inside out before you go anywhere near you own money.

You should be looking at the long view of a particular currency for example looking at the 4 hour graph and seeing the big picture. It's easy to look at the 5 minute graph or even the 1 minute and think the market is going one way when in fact the whole market could be going in the opposite direction.

Learning to know when to stop and pull out of an investment is also a very important tool to master.

You can set stop loss - SL markers which will cut your losses at a certain point. Learning where to put these is key. But learning WHEN to enter the trade will allow you the minimum stop loss position. You want to allow the trade to breathe.

You can also put in TP – Take Profit makers too so that when this is hit you have taken the amount of pips you wanted to and the position would close.

Once you begin trading I highly recommend using only 2p/2 Cents to trade with. A very low spread allows you a lot of room to move and loses will be very low. This will allow you to get used to trading money.

Ultimately trading is about continually learning about the Forex market and learning what drives the markets and through patience you will succeed.

Finally if you enjoyed this book please leave a review.

Good luck friends and trade wisely.

Charles